This book belongs

God Loves You
Proverbs from the Bible

CONTEMPORARY ENGLISH VERSION

ABS

AMERICAN BIBLE SOCIETY
NEW YORK

Printed in the United States of America
Eng. Sel. CEV880P-105161
ABS-6/00-6,000-46,000—H3(6)

Illustrated by Lynn Adams
Book design by Malle Whitaker

ABOUT THIS BOOK

Do you ever think about being wise? To be wise is to know the difference between right and wrong and between good and bad. People who are wise are people with wisdom.

Proverbs are sayings that will teach you how to live right so that you may become wise. Proverbs will also teach you about trusting in God.

Wisdom is like a teacher or guide leading you along the path of knowledge. This book of Proverbs is your roadmap. Are you ready to begin the journey?

> If you are already wise,
>   you will become even wiser.
> And if you are smart,
>   you will learn to understand
> proverbs and sayings,
> as well as words of wisdom
>   and all kinds of riddles.
>   *Proverbs 1.5-6*

Many proverbs are short. They are fun to learn and easy to remember.

You will be glad
    that you know these sayings
        and can recite them.

Proverbs 22.18

Grow in God's love! God loves you and wants you

- to become wise
- to be happy
- to be kind to others, and
- to trust in God.

GOD LOVES YOU
and
Wants You To Become
Wise

Honey is good for you,
my children,
        and it tastes sweet.
Wisdom is like honey
        for your life—
if you find it,
        your future is bright.

Proverbs 24.13, 14

8

Search for wisdom
as you would search for silver
or hidden treasure.
Then you will understand
what it means to respect
and to know the LORD God.

Proverbs 2.4, 5

9

All wisdom comes from the LORD,
and so do common sense
and understanding.

♦ ♦ ♦ ♦

With wisdom you will learn
what is right
and honest and fair.

Proverbs 2.6, 9

10

On this earth four things
    are small but very wise:
Ants, who seem to be feeble,
but store up food
    all summer long;
badgers, who seem to be weak,
    but live among the rocks;
locusts, who have no king,
    but march like an army;
lizards, which can be caught
in your hand,
    but sneak into palaces.

Proverbs 30.24-28

If you value Wisdom and hold tightly to her,
   great honors will be yours.
It will be like wearing a glorious crown
   of beautiful flowers.

Proverbs 4.8, 9

12

GOD LOVES YOU
and
Wants to Guide You
in Every Way

The Law of the Lord is a lamp,
and its teachings
        shine brightly.
Correction and self-control
        will lead you through life.

Proverbs 6.23

14

My child, obey the teachings
of your parents,
and wear their teachings
as you would a lovely hat
or a pretty necklace.

Proverbs 1.8, 9

15

My child, use common sense
and sound judgment!
    Always keep them in mind.
They will help you to live
    a long and beautiful life.
You will walk safely
    and never stumble;
you will rest without a worry
    and sleep soundly.

Proverbs 3.21-24

16

The lifestyle of good people
is like sunlight at dawn
that keeps getting brighter
until broad daylight.
The lifestyle of the wicked
is like total darkness,
and they will never know
what makes them stumble.

Proverbs 4.18, 19

17

Good people have kind thoughts,
but you should never trust
    the advice of someone evil.
Bad advice is a deadly trap,
but good advice
    is like a shield.

Proverbs 12.5, 6

If you have good sense,
instruction will help you
   to have even better sense.
And if you live right,
education will help you
   to know even more.

Proverbs 9.9

19

Good people live right,
and God blesses the children
who follow their example.

Proverbs 20.7

20

GOD LOVES YOU
and
Wants You To Be
Happy

Try hard to do right,
and you will win friends;
go looking for trouble,
and you will find it.

Proverbs 11.27

22

I't's healthy to be content,
but envy can eat you up.
Proverbs 14.30

Troublemakers get in trouble,
and their terrible anger
    will get them nowhere.
                    Proverbs 22.8

Don't be a fool
and quickly lose your temper —
be sensible and patient.

Proverbs 29.11

25

Sneering at others is a spark
that sets a city on fire;
using good sense can put out
the flames of anger.

Proverbs 29.8

26

Gossip is no good!
It causes hard feelings
    and comes between friends.

Proverbs 16.28

Kind words are like honey—
they cheer you up
    and make you feel strong.
                Proverbs 16.24

28

Don't brag about tomorrow!
Each day brings
    its own surprises.
Don't brag about yourself—
    let others praise you.

Proverbs 27.1, 2

29

Lazy people can learn
     by watching an anthill.
Ants don't have leaders,
but they store up food
     during harvest season.

Proverbs 6.6-8

GOD LOVES YOU
and
Wants You To Be Kind
to Others

The LORD sees everything,
whether good or bad.
Kind words are good medicine,
but deceitful words
can really hurt.

Proverbs 15.3, 4

32

We may think we are doing
the right thing,
but the LORD always knows
what is in our hearts.
Doing what is right and fair
pleases the LORD
more than an offering.

Proverbs 21.2, 3

If you obey the Lord,
you will always know
     the right thing to say.
But no one will trust you
     if you tell lies.

Proverbs 10.32

Truth will last forever;
    lies are soon found out.
An evil mind is deceitful,
but gentle thoughts
    bring happiness.

Proverbs 12.19, 20

35

A messenger you can trust
is just as refreshing
    as cool water in summer.
Broken promises
are worse than rain clouds
    that don't bring rain.

Proverbs 25.13, 14

36

Do all you can for everyone
who deserves your help.
Don't tell your neighbor
to come back tomorrow,
if you can help today.

Proverbs 3.27, 28

37

Hatred stirs up trouble;
love overlooks the wrongs
that others do.

Proverbs 10.12

38

You will keep your friends
if you forgive them,
but you will lose your friends
if you keep talking about
what they did wrong.

Proverbs 17.9

39

The LORD blesses everyone who
freely gives food to the poor.

Proverbs 22.9

Giving an honest answer
is a sign
of true friendship.

Proverbs 24.26

If you try to be kind and good,
you will be blessed with life
and goodness and honor.

Proverbs 21.21

42

TRUST IN GOD
because
GOD LOVES YOU

If you know what you're doing,
you will prosper.
God blesses everyone
who trusts him.

Proverbs 16.20

44

With all your heart
you must trust the LORD
 and not your own judgment.
Always let him lead you,
and he will clear the road
 for you to follow.

Proverbs 3.5, 6

My child, listen carefully
     to everything I say.
Don't forget a single word,
     but think about it all.
Knowing these teachings
will mean true life
     and good health for you.
Carefully guard your thoughts
because they are the source
     of true life.
Never tell lies or be deceitful
     in what you say.
Keep looking straight ahead,
     without turning aside.
Know where you are headed,
and you will stay
     on solid ground.

Proverbs 4.20-26

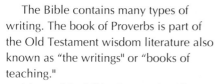

WHAT ARE PROVERBS?

The Bible contains many types of writing. The book of Proverbs is part of the Old Testament wisdom literature also known as "the writings" or "books of teaching."

Many of the biblical proverbs offer advice regarding individual behavior in daily life. While the writings go back to the time of ancient Israel, they offer guidance for life today for both young and old — and those in between!

Wise sayings, or proverbs, are a part of many cultures. Often they are cited as morals, or lessons to be learned from a particular experience. Some proverbs that may be familiar to children are from the fables of Aesop, a Greek writer who lived c. 620-560 B.C.

No act of kindness, no matter how small, is ever wasted.
The Lion and The Mouse –

Slow and steady wins the race.
The Hare and The Tortoise –

Some other familiar proverbs or sayings were written by the Chinese philosopher, Confucius, who lived 551-479 B.C.

When you have faults, do not fear to abandon them.

Have no friends not equal to yourself.

A well-known saying by the civil rights leader, the Rev. Dr. Martin Luther King, Jr. (1929-1968) is:

Injustice anywhere is a threat to justice everywhere.
Letter from a Birmingham Jail, 1963 –

Like these sayings, many of the biblical proverbs focus on moral teachings. Many others deal with religious teachings. For the most part, the biblical proverbs go back to the time of King Solomon, one of the great kings of Israel.

The Proverbs in the Bible are written in poetic style. A typical proverb takes the form of a short verse in which the first half states the theme and the second half echoes it. For example,

**Work hard,
and you will have a lot of food;** (theme)
**waste time,
and you will have a lot of trouble.** (echo)
Proverbs 28.19

Because most of the Proverbs are short, they are easy to remember. What makes the Bible's proverbs so popular is that they make such powerful statements with very few words.

HOW TO USE THIS BOOK

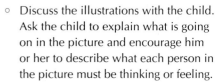

GOD LOVES YOU: Proverbs from the Bible offers an interesting and fun way to introduce children to the importance of wisdom and instruction, the value of hard work and honesty, and how to get along with others. At the heart of the proverbs is learning to grow in God's love and to trust in God. The delightful illustrations that accompany the Scripture passages are designed to enhance the biblical message.

This book is designed for children ages 5-7. To help them get the most out of this book, we suggest that you participate in a learning experience with them in the following ways:

○ Read the text out loud to a young child or allow an older child to read it out loud to you. The Scripture passages are translated from the original Hebrew text into the kinds of words and phrases children are familiar with.

○ Show the child where the passages are found in your own Bible.

○ Talk with the child about what the proverbs mean and encourage the child to talk about experiences in his/her own life that the proverbs may bring to mind.

○ Talk with the child about the difference between wisdom and foolishness. Together, try to think of someone who behaves wisely. Think of everyday things someone might do that would be foolish. Be careful not to ridicule the child's friends or embarrass the child.

○ Discuss the illustrations with the child. Ask the child to explain what is going on in the picture and encourage him or her to describe what each person in the picture must be thinking or feeling.

○ Encourage the child to memorize proverbs that he or she finds especially meaningful. Ask the child to write the proverb on drawing or poster paper and to draw a picture to illustrate the proverb.

○ Discuss with the child what it means to trust in God. Ask the child to describe how the proverbs show that God loves him/her. You may wish to use this opportunity to discuss personal safety and when it is appropriate and not appropriate to trust someone.

It is our hope and prayer that children will enjoy using this Scripture Portion and will be encouraged to begin a lifetime habit of reading the Bible. Other attractive books and activity materials which use the *Contemporary English Version* are available from the American Bible Society. Write for a catalog today and let us know what kinds of Scripture resources you like to use with young children.

48